CONTENTS

WHAT IS RESISTANCE?

B Y LATE 1941, the Second World War was in its third year and Hitler's plan to exterminate the Jewish race was taking shape. Jews from all over Europe were being transported to concentration camps and sealed ghettos. If they didn't die in the transports they were gassed or worked to death. Many were massacred by Einsatzgruppen (mobile units of soldiers) in the woods of the Ukraine, or shot on arrival in Poland. The borders of Poland and Germany were closed and, fearful of waves of penniless, Jewish refugees, most countries not occupied by German troops had limited the numbers of Jews that they would take in. In the following four years all that the Jews and the other minority groups that the Nazis had targeted could

Above: Infantrymen marching in Nuremberg, Germany in 1937.

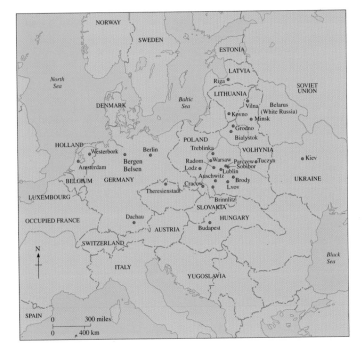

Left: Map of Europe showing some of the major places where rebellions or acts of resistance took place.

The ultimate sacrifice

Samuel Pisar lived in the Bialystok ghetto in Poland. In 1943, as the Germans liquidated the ghetto he hid with 30 others in a cellar:

'...my teacher...Professor Bergman was rocking his infant son, trying to stop his coughing. On the other side of the trapdoor above us came the shouts of German search parties and the barking of their dogs.

We all fell silent; only the baby's coughing

continued ... A man crawled over and put his hand over the baby's mouth. The coughing ceased. Minutes passed. The child sank limply to the ground.

All the while Professor Bergman sat petrified. I knew he was not a coward. Even then, I understood that if he could think or feel anything at all, he was weighing one life against thirty, even if that life was his own son's.'

(Quoted in Martin Gilbert, *The Holocaust*)

do was try and survive or escape or, under the most adverse conditions, fight back.

Countries, armed with all the machinery of war were buckling under the German onslaught. It is therefore all the more remarkable that under such terrible circumstances people fought back.

During these years Jews hid, escaped and bribed their way out of Germany. Many worked in the labour and death camps and ghettos. They wrote down what they had witnessed, kept secret radios, published pamphlets and documents, held secret religious services, helped other Jews to escape, stole food and brought comfort to their families and friends. Other nationalities – Poles, Germans, the French, Italians, Bulgarians and Dutch – individually sheltered Jews at great risk to their own lives and those of their families. Many occupied states prevented the deportation of their Jews. All of the people and countries that helped the Jews could be said to have resisted the Holocaust.

Below: Jews from Bialystok being marched away – probably to Auschwitz death camp.

Armed Resistance

It has been estimated that 1.5 million Jews took part in armed resistance against the Germans, many of them dying in the process and provoking massive reprisals against their families and communities. Jews fought in the French resistance movement, among Polish and Soviet resistance groups in the woods of Poland, Belarus and Ukraine and in the ghettos and the death camps. There was even a Jewish resistance group, the *Baumgruppe* operating in Berlin, Germany, until 1942.

Those Jews who chose to fight faced terrible adversity. Many of them fought after months or even years on starvation rations, gruelling forced labour, and many more years of rejection and hatred by the state they had believed they were citizens of. They had few weapons and no support from the Allied forces. Some faced anti-Semitism from those who, like them, were enemies of Germany, but were scared of reprisal. Most of those who fought against the German regime knew that if they were discovered helping Jews they would suffer at best immediate death and at worst days of torture when they might be forced to betray their comrades. They knew that terrible reprisals would be made not just against their families but against their whole community.

Below: Werner Steinbrink and Edith Fraenkel, members of the Baumgruppe, a group of young Communists who operated in Berlin until May 1942 when they were captured and shot. They organized anti-Nazi poster campaigns and destroyed an anti-Soviet exhibition in Berlin.

Worse still than all of these things was the overwhelming superiority of those that they fought. Very often the Jews' best hope was not that they could defeat their enemies but that their deaths might frustrate their enemies' aims or cause temporary inconvenience.

Below: The Vilna ghetto community organized theatrical and musical performances such as this one.

The Vilna Ghetto 1943

The dilemma of those Jews who wished to fight the Nazis can be seen in the events surrounding one breakout from the ghetto of Vilna in Lithuania in 1943. A group of young people got hold of guns and joined a partisan group in the Narotch Forest nearby. They engaged the Germans in battle just outside the city and several of them were captured. When the Germans learned that they were Jewish escapees, every member of their families and the leaders of all the work parties that they came from were shot. Afterwards the entire ghetto was divided into work parties of ten. If one person disappeared the rest of their work party would die. The Vilna ghetto newspaper called those who had run away to fight 'traitors to the Jewish people' and said that the idealistic thing to do in the ghetto was to stay in it and not risk the lives of the 20,000 other Jews who could not escape.

Dying as an act of resistance

There were many other ways to resist the Nazi goal of the annihilation of the Jewish race than fighting, running away or surviving. Part of the German strategy with the Jews was to do as much as possible to make them feel less than human. In the camps people were tattooed with numbers, given inadequate uniforms, were underfed and had their possessions taken and their hair cut off. Primo Levi, a survivor of Auschwitz has written about this drive to dehumanize the Jews and sees the challenge to maintain a sense of self as a way of resisting and thwarting the Nazi goals. Everyone who maintained a sense of identity or religion in the face of some of the most horrific things that one human being could do to another was resisting the Holocaust, even if he or she died in the death camps.

Some people even chose death when they might have survived. A survivor, Szymon Datner, recalls one man, a carter (wheelmaker), who was being taken to the transports with his family and was urged by his wife to run away – which he could easily have done. But he refused to leave his family and went to the Treblinka death camp with them. Other stories recall adults volunteering to go to the gas chambers with orphaned children, and nurses accompanying their patients to the camps when they might have stayed behind.

Below: One way of humiliating the Jews was to force them to wear an identifying yellow star of David. Some Jews wore it with shame while others wore it proudly.

Left: Shmuel Zygielbojm lived in Warsaw with his wife and family until 1939. A socialist member of the Jewish Council, he advocated passive resistance to the forced movement of Warsaw's Jews into a ghetto area.

Shmuel Zygielbojm

Shmuel Zygielbojm was a Polish Jew from Warsaw who was sent to London in 1940 to represent the interests of the Polish Jews in London. He became a leading speaker and made the fate of the Jews known to as many people in London as would listen. In 1943, after the Warsaw ghetto uprising he committed suicide in London. His suicide note explained that he had not been fortunate enough to die with his comrades in Warsaw with weapons in their hands. He had felt he could no longer live while the Jewish people were being annihilated. His letter concluded 'By my death I wish to express my vigorous protest against the apathy with which the world regards and resigns itself to the slaughter of the Jewish people.'

SURVIVING THE HOLOCAUST

Escape and hiding

BY 1933 many Jews living in Germany and Poland chose to leave for places which they hoped would be safer – Austria, France, Holland, Belgium. As Hitler's plans for the Jews became clearer, 300,000 people – 30 per cent of the Jewish population of Germany – had left their country by 1939. In Poland about 400,000 Jews had emigrated by 1939.

After 1939, as Germany invaded and occupied more countries, the number of Jews living in German occupied territories swelled by two million and two years later with the invasion of Russia three million more came under German control. Escape was impossible for such huge numbers, and those remaining in Germany were either shipped into Poland to live in the ghettos or found some way to live within Germany. Many were disguised as Gentiles (non-Jews); some were hidden by kind neighbours or by people who took money to hide them. Some were disguised as *Mischling* (half Jews or those married to Germans). Even for the estimated 5,000 Jews who lived in hiding in Berlin, life carried a

Below: A wedding photo of a Jewish couple, Herman de Leeuw and Annie Pais, taken in Amsterdam in 1942. Only one of the people in the photograph, Samual Schrivjer (sixth from the left), survived the war.

Life in hiding

With the help of Gentile friends, Bronisawa Goldfischer survived the war. The events she describes here took place when she was 13 years old and living in Lwow, Poland.

'In December 1942 it was obvious that sooner or later all the Jews in the ghetto would be eliminated. In the face of this my father decided to save at least me, found a place for me with a Polish family whom he paid 15,000 zlotys… Despite the danger they were in because of me – they risked their own lives by taking me in – they looked after me like I was one of their own children, and it was thanks to them that I survived.

(One day an intelligence agent came to Bronisawa's house) … he said I was very good at playing the part of an Aryan girl. Then he searched the wardrobe and to his surprise he found a photograph of me in a special dress kneeling down to take Communion. My parents had had that photograph taken in the ghetto by a photographer they knew… This obviously misled the agent because he asked me a few more questions about my papers and left.'

(Quoted in Maria Hochberg-Mariañska and Noe Grüss, *The Children Accuse*).

constant threat of discovery or betrayal by their neighbours once their money had run out. In German occupied territories it is thought that 200,000 Jews survived in hiding.

After 1939 small numbers of European Jews continued to escape across Europe to the unoccupied region of France which was self-governing. From there about 12,000 were brought into Portugal or by sea to Casablanca. 20,000 found their way to Shanghai in China while 4,000 escaped to Kobe in Japan. 13,000 German Jews with enough capital to prove they would not be a burden on their new home were able to get visas for Britain or Palestine. Until the invasion of Russia, the Nazis were still willing to allow emigration at a price.

Below: In 1936 these Parisian Jews lived peaceful lives within French society. This was soon to change.

Betrayal and Rescue

It was German policy from the 1930s onwards to 'Aryanize' Jewish property. By that they meant confiscate it and give it to German citizens – and later – citizens of German occupied territories such as France and Poland. This gave an incentive to ordinary people – neighbours and friends of the Jews, to betray them to the authorities. Anyone seen to be a friend of the Jews was a traitor and could suffer terribly. The Nazis perfected their incentives to encourage betrayal of the Jews: they persuaded people to give Jews up by saying that they might get the house of the person they betrayed. The alternative was, if they helped them, to go to the gas chambers with them.

On the other hand vast numbers of people, for many different reasons, risked their lives to help the Jews: anti-Semitic Polish nationalists because they wished to stop the Nazis grow in

Below: Like millions of other Jews, the survival of this man and child depended on the sympathy of strangers, chance or their own limited ability to protect themselves.

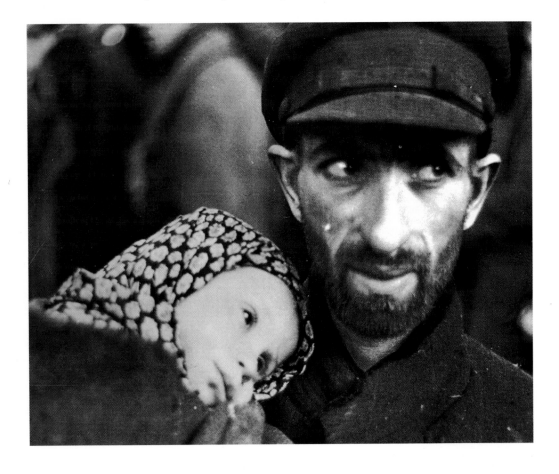

Rabbi Solomon Schonfeld

As early as 1933 the young and charismatic Rabbi Schonfeld could see that the Jews of Europe were in terrible danger. He lived and looked after a congregation in North London and had access to Jewish families that would take in Jewish refugees, especially children. At that time Britain would only allow in a small number of Jews, and only on the guarantee that a British person would provide for them. From the mid-1930s he began bringing groups of refugees into Britain, using his friends and congregation as guarantors. They were housed at first in his own house, in the school he had established, and later in refugee hostels. One of his brothers tells the story of how on his return home from university he found a child asleep in his bed with another sleeping under it! The war brought an end to his efforts, as it meant that refugees couldn't travel to Britain, and he spent the war years caring for the children that he had brought over. After the war he travelled around Poland, looking for orphan children. It is estimated that Rabbi Schonfeld rescued about 3,500 Jews, mostly children.

power; Christians because they believed the Nazis' actions were wrong and unChristian; neighbours and strangers in exchange for cash or out of pity. In Chambon-sur-Lignon in France, the entire town formed an underground transport system to smuggle Jews to safety. In Holland there was a two-day general strike in opposition to Nazi policies towards the Jews, which ended in terrible punishments for those involved. Towards the end of the war many people, apathetic or too scared to help during the Holocaust, suddenly realized that sheltering a few Jews might help them at the end of the war, when they might be called to account for their lack of action.

Right: Solomon Schonfeld with some of the children he rescued.

The Frank Family

Otto Frank and his family were German Jews who left Germany in 1933 when the Nazi rise to power began. They lived openly in Amsterdam through the German invasion and the imposition of anti-Jewish laws, until 1942 when transportations of Jews to the death and concentration camps began. They went into hiding in a secret annexe above Otto's business premises. They planned their period of hiding in advance and made all the necessary arrangements for money and help. They chose not to leave Amsterdam for a 'safe' country and remained together as a family, despite the terrible dangers.

For two years, Otto, his wife and two daughters Anne and Margot lived in hiding with another Jewish family, the Pels and a family friend, Pfeffer. They had to remain completely hidden at all

Below: Newly arrived Jewish women at Auschwitz in 1944. Anne Frank, her mother and sister would also have gone through the process of having their hair shaved off.

Anne Frank's diary

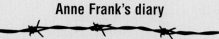

Shut up inside the attic, Anne's only contacts with the outside world were the people that her family relied on to bring them food. Her diary entries are about quarrels, her growing love for Peter Pels, and occasionally, anti-Semitism and the war. Here she writes about her sadness:

'I wander from one room to another, downstairs and up again, feeling like a song bird whose wings have been brutally clipped and who is beating itself in utter darkness against the bars on its cage. "Go outside, laugh, take a breath of fresh air," a voice cries within me, but I don't even feel a response any more; I go and lie on the divan and sleep, to make the time pass more quickly, and the stillness and the terrible fear, because there is no way of killing them.'

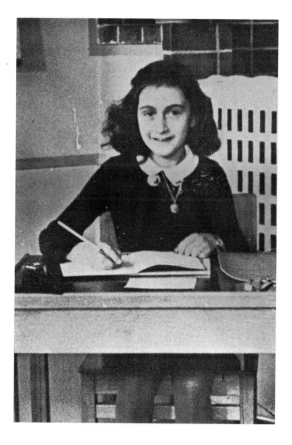

Below: Anne in happier days – aged 11 at school.

times, being careful that they made no noises, which might arouse suspicions. The youngest daughter, Anne, whiled away the 25 months of hiding by writing a diary addressed to an imaginary friend, Kitty. She developed a relationship with Peter Pels, who was two years older than her. Strains emerged between the two families in the difficult conditions they were forced to live in. They had a radio and heard news of what was going on in the war. Anne even listened to a British broadcast describing the gas chambers. Otto's employees and friends risked their own lives to bring the Franks food. Finally the Franks were discovered or perhaps betrayed. They spent a few weeks in Westerbork transit camp in Holland and were then transported to Auschwitz, where Mrs Frank and Mrs Pels died. Anne and Margot were transferred to Bergen-Belsen where both of them died of typhoid.

Surviving in the ghettos

The ghettos of Poland and occupied Russia were created as a short-term way of containing the millions of Jews until they could be shipped to slave labour or death camps. The most run-down, unsanitary sections of the larger towns were walled off, and all Jews were given a few days to find accommodation within these ghetto areas. At first the ghettos were open, but by 1942 most were sealed. Telephones and radios were removed, parks and open spaces were all outside the walls, there was little or no sanitation or running water and people quickly grew too tired and hungry to observe even the minimum of cleanliness. Fuel was scarce and rations consisted of about 1,100 calories per person at best, often consisting of spoiled food rejected by the outside community – largely sour bread, turnips and potatoes. Most families were lucky to have a single room to themselves.

Those who had managed to smuggle valuables into the ghetto fared better. In many ghettos they were able to buy exemption from forced labour while their funds lasted, and they could buy black market food, or extra food, smuggled in by poorer people.

Below: Between 1939 and 1945 people did many desperate things in order to survive. Here a group of wealthy Poles are cutting up a dead horse in order to survive a siege in Warsaw.

Left: Abandoned Jewish children begging in the ghetto streets of Warsaw 1941.

Orphans in the ghetto

The increase in numbers of orphans in the ghettos was horrific. By November 1941 there were 10,000 orphaned children living in the Warsaw ghetto. About 2,000 of them lived in orphanages set up by the Jewish Councils. The other 8,000 lived on the street. By 1942, 25,000 children were in institutions within the ghetto and 75,000 lived in the streets where they formed gangs, begged or found some way of making a living – selling cigarettes or sweets, smuggling or doing odd jobs. Survival for these children depended on luck and judgement. The children's centres set up by the Nazis were not safe places, since their objective was to keep the children together where they could be easily transported. One orphaned survivor was Zbyseck, a cigarette seller. 'Everybody I was with died in 1941. I travel around, occasionally pinching something. The day before yesterday some kids set on me so I punched one on the nose till he cried and then I tripped the other one and he ran... No-one jokes with me.'

(From Zieman Joseph, *The Cigarette Sellers of Three Crosses Square*. Quoted in Ruby Rohrlich (ed), *Resisting the Holocaust*)

People quickly began to die from hunger in the ghettos. 11,000 in Warsaw in 1941 alone. They also began to die from typhus, heart disease, dysentery, TB and gastro-enteritis.

But just as quickly, people learned how to survive, by making things to sell outside, opening cafes and shops inside, forging work permits, making clothes, boots – anything they could turn their hands to. Where there was soil, small plots of vegetables were grown. Smuggling quickly developed with children often being the ones sent outside the ghettos to buy food on the black market, while the parents worked in the slave factories. People learned to hide from the squads who daily came into the ghetto looking for workers for forced labour. Early warning systems were set up giving people time to hide or escape the Nazis searching the buildings. Strangely there was a boom in marriages in the ghetto as both young people and old came to realize that to survive, the family unit was stronger than being alone. Religious and cultural organizations developed, people played instruments, sang, put on plays in the evenings. Above all they co-operated with the Germans since this was their only guarantee of survival.

Below: a German soldier patrols the Kracow ghetto looking for people to fill the transports to the death camps. If people were discovered without their documents, they could be dragged off to the transports.

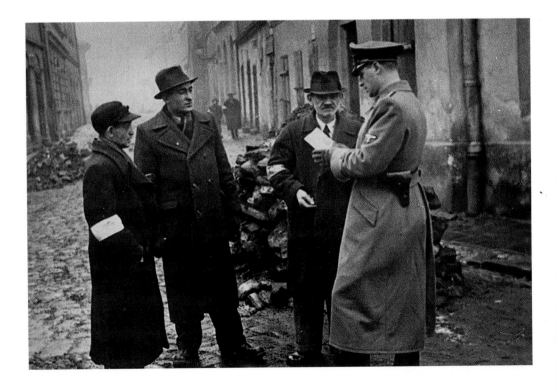

A Hanukkah celebration in the Lodz ghetto

'Hunger, cold and conflicts were all forgotten. Shoemakers and tailors, physicians, lawyers and pharmacists, all at one, we were one big family. That could not have happened in Berlin... but here, behind the barbed wire, something existed that united us all – our Jewishness. When they sang together, they forgot their suffering and misery; they were still alive and in song they praised God, who many times before had performed miracles. When they sang about the little lamp whose oil for one day lasted eight, the singers regained their courage and their hope.'

(Ruth Alton's testimony, Leo Baeck Institute Archives, quoted in Lucy Dawidowitz, *The War against the Jews*)

The Judenrat

Very few Germans policed the ghettos. Once inside the ghettos the Judenrat, the Jewish Council, had to follow Nazi orders and run the ghettos. For the most part the Judenrat and the Jewish police were just people pulled out of the crowd and forced on pain of death to do the work. They collected taxes, maintained files on addresses and numbers of Jews and administered the rationing. They even provided a police force to lead first the destitute and criminals, then the children, the sick and old, and then the exhausted skilled workers to the transports to the slave and death camps. The Jewish officials justified their actions by claiming that by sending the required number of Jews to the transports they were saving the lives of the others. Others simply did it to save their own families.

Below: These men in the Warsaw ghetto were lined up and searched some time in 1943, during the violent ghetto uprising of that year.

Surviving in the Forests

Thousands of Jews fleeing from the sudden, massive German advance into the Baltic states in June 1941 found refuge in the woods around the borders of Poland, Belarus, Lithuania and Ukraine. They were joined by hundreds of Russian soldiers escaping from advancing Germans, as well as civilians unwilling to be shipped to Germany to work as slaves in the factories. The Jewish partisan groups that formed, besides taking part in guerrilla attacks, also sheltered the many Jews who were scattered and helpless in the woods. One group in particular, the Bielski Otriad, took in every Jewish person who they found wandering in the woods. Jews were lucky to find the group. Polish and Russian partisan groups were just as likely to murder them for their possessions. The Bielski group numbered several thousands. Its members lived in a settlement deep in the Nolibocka forest where they set up a gun repair shop, meat processing factory and boot factory. Craftsmen used the materials they found in the forests to supply most of their needs. At first they raided local farms for food, but they were soon trading repaired and stolen guns with other partisan groups for food. A very primitive social system emerged – with those who had been businessmen in Berlin or Warsaw almost useless to the group,

Below: The Bielski Otriad, a Jewish partisan group which operated successfully until liberation by Russian troops. Simple peasants, the Bielski brothers knew how to survive in the forests and were responsible for the rescue of over a thousand Jews.

while simple peasant farmers like the Bielski brothers organized and ruled the community. Of the intellectuals who made it into the woods, only doctors, dentists and nurses were of any use to the group. Despite this everyone was given rations. In this way, city folk who had no hope of surviving alone in the forest made it to the end of the war.

Above: Many other partisan groups operated in the same forest as the Bielski group, but few of them tolerated Jews.

Children in the forests

Many people were never fortunate enough to find a group like the Bielski Otriad. In March 1943, a 12-year-old boy called Matti Drobless escaped from the Warsaw ghetto with his older sister and younger brother:

'Our survival was based on our will to live and the talents we adopted. We stole food from the farms and removed articles of clothing from the washlines. We scrounged and when there was no alternative we sent our youngest brother into homes to beg. We taught him prayers and instructed him to pose as a Polish war orphan…

…We never met another Jew in our wanderings through the forests.'

(Quoted in Martin Gilbert, *The Holocaust: The Jewish Tragedy*)

Surviving the camps

By October 1941 mass deportations of Jews to specially built death camps in Poland had begun. Some of these camps, such as Auschwitz, also contained factories and mines where slave labour was used. On arrival at the camps as many as 80 per cent of the Jews from the transports were immediately murdered. Others survived – doctors, nurses, dentists and technicians were useful in running the camp, and musicians were often sent to the camp orchestra. Others were able to survive in indoor assignments such as the factories. But much of the work consisted of hard manual labour: mining and building and quarrying. Most people quickly perished in the Polish winters.

A 'privileged' position for prisoners was the sonderkommando – the men selected to work in the gas chambers sorting through dead bodies and discarded clothes. They had extra rations and good clothes. But they knew that they would die since their first task on being selected was to take the previous sonderkommando to the gas chambers. Others, usually criminals, were made into kapos, people who supervised the work of the slave labourers. They had many privileges in return for their brutal treatment of the other inmates.

Below: Auschwitz death camp and its satellite camps remain as a testimony to the countless people who died there.

Mengele's experiments

Most bizarrely of all, some people survived because they were selected for medical experimentation – although thousands more died horrific deaths as a result of the experiments of men like Dr Joseph Mengele. The only way that Jewish children under the age of ten survived the initial selections was by being taken for Mengele's experiments. Ernest Spiegel and his twin sister were chosen for the experiments. He was put in charge of a barracks of twin boys. In 1944 there were about 200 still surviving, relatively well looked after and waiting to be chosen for experimentation. On a visit in October of that year by a high ranking Nazi the children were nearly sent to the gas chambers but were spared when Mengele intervened. When Auschwitz was evacuated in 1945, 33 sets of twins survived.

Strangely, illness saved some people. Minor illnesses were treated in the camp hospitals and in them the sick had a chance to recover a little strength. This was a risky business though since patients ran the constant risk of being selected for the gas chambers. When Poland was liberated, those in Auschwitz who were too sick to be included in the death marches westward (the Germans' attempts to escape from the advancing Allies) were abandoned in the camp and so were found by the Russian troops.

Above: Eva and Miriam Moses were selected to take part in the experiments of Dr Mengele and so survived their years in Auschwitz while most of their family perished.

Just as important as physical survival was psychological survival. Most people lost their families in the selections and gave up in despair, becoming what the camp inmates called *Musselmen*, zombie-like figures who had lost all hope or sense of identity and died quickly. Others were able to form new relationships within their work parties and found support in that way. Some were inspired by their religion, while for others the determination to survive kept them going.

Surviving the death marches

By January 1945 German troops were in retreat across Russia, and the death camps of Poland were threatened with liberation. Rather than have the evidence of the previous five years fall into Allied hands, the Germans evacuated the death camps, and vast numbers of malnourished people were forced to walk hundreds of miles into German territory. The marches were chaotic. No preparations were made for transporting such huge numbers of people. Those who straggled were shot. They took place in the dead of winter and surviving them must have taken an amazing act of will. At the end of the marches thousands were crammed into camps that were horrifically over-crowded, even by German standards of camp life. Typhoid epidemics broke out, people starved to death, there was even evidence of cannibalism among the desperate inmates.

Ironically, death came to many of the German concentration camp inmates after liberation. Allied soldiers, stunned by what they encountered, offered oatmeal, sugar, salt, dried milk powder and tinned meat – food which was too rich for the starving inmates. Typhoid carried off others. At Bergen-Belsen 300 people died each day after liberation.

Right: Dachau concentration camp in April 1945, shortly after liberation.

Below: Thousands of starving Jews were herded to Bergen-Belsen at the end of the death marches. Anne Frank and her sister Margot died of typhoid in the camp. This picture shows conditions after liberation in 1945.

The luck of Sim Kessel

Sim Kessel was a French boxer who was caught smuggling arms for the French resistance. He eventually found himself working in the mines at Jaworzno, a satellite camp of Auschwitz in Poland. His chances of surviving such work were tiny and he was eventually selected to go to the gas chambers. Standing naked with the other emaciated men in the snow, waiting to be marched off to his death, he noticed that one of the SS men had a broken nose and scars across his eyes, typical signs of an ex-boxer. Kessel walked up to him and said one word in German 'boxer'. The guard saw Kessel's own boxing scars and asked him about his matches. Suddenly he ordered Kessel, still naked, to get on his motorcycle. Kessel obeyed and the guard took him to the hospital. Later, on a death march, Kessel was put in an open freight car and made to lie down for five days, tangled up with 70 other men. When the two men beside him died Kessel took their blankets and burrowed beneath their corpses to keep out the biting winter winds. Only nine people of the 70 in his freight car survived.

RESCUE FROM HOME AND ABROAD

The fate of the Jews in the occupied states of Europe

AUSTRIA AND Czechoslovakia conformed to German policy almost as soon as they were invaded and initiated anti-Jewish legislation and controls over Jewish activities and life. By the end of the war, all Austrian and Czech Jews still surviving were either *Mischling* (half or quarter Jewish) or had survived in hiding. In France the pro-Nazi Vichy government deported all Jewish refugees to the death camps, and later even French Jews were deported. Belgium and Holland also gave up their Jews. Rumania probably had the worst record of murder, enacting its own anti-Jewish legislation long before German troops reached it, carrying out pogroms (mass murder) and deportations. In Yugoslavia and Greece most of the Jewish population perished. Hungary took in many refugees from Germany, Czechoslovakia and Poland and although there were deportations and pogroms most Jews remained relatively safe until Hungary was invaded in 1943. Deportations began then on a massive scale.

Below: Jewish deportees arriving at Theresienstadt ghetto in Czechoslovakia. Thirty thousand Jews from Berlin, Vienna and Prague died there and many more were deported to the death camps from there.

Left: These German Jews are being deported from Wurzburg in Germany, probably to the Lublin ghetto in Poland.

Despite this tragic record, many countries tried to help the Jews. Luxembourg enabled many Jews to escape as far as France and Portugal. To their credit, Italy, a fascist state, was reluctant to give up its Jews. No Italian Jews were deported until 1943 when Germany invaded Italy. By that time many Jews had been helped to leave or had gone into hiding. In Bulgaria, one of Germany's allies, Jews were at first subject to anti-Semitic laws and 11,000 were deported to Poland, but after public protests no more deportations were made. In Norway the Norwegian resistance helped about half the Jewish population to escape into Sweden. In Denmark almost all of Denmark's 8,000 Jews were ferried to Sweden. Finland also refused to give up its 2,000 Jews.

Divisiòn Espanöa de Voluntarios

Between 1941 and 1943 a division of 40,000 Spanish soldiers served on the Russian front within the German army. But the Spaniards did not share the Nazi view of Jews, Slavs and Russians as *Untermenschen* (members of an inferior race) and treated all people that they encountered with respect. The Spanish troops never actually opposed German treatment of Jews in the towns in which they were based, but they did not help carry out German policy. In the Spanish military hospitals, Jews and Slavs received treatment and Jewish nurses and orderlies were protected from the constant demands for Jews for the transports to the death camps. Spanish protection was short-lived though. When the Spanish troops were withdrawn in 1943 all the Jews they had been protecting went back to the ghettos.

Individual acts of heroism

While millions of people turned their backs on Jewish suffering, thousands of individuals risked their lives to help, some of whom came from very unusual backgrounds. One unexpected source of help for fleeing Jews came from a Polish thief. When the Lwow ghetto was being emptied and its Jews being sent to death camps in June 1943, several people escaped into the sewers where they had no way of surviving. While they were lost they encountered Leopold Socha who used the sewers for smuggling. He took them to a dry hiding place in the sewers and brought food every day. Each week he brought clean clothes. Of the 21 people who Socha hid, ten survived a year in the sewers and emerged on liberation. According to one of the people whom he had helped, a young Jewish woman called Halina Wind, Socha was hated by his neighbours for helping the Jews.

Left: Jewish partisan groups survived in the forests around Poland, Belarus and Lithuania. Few of them survived the war. This group consists of refugees from Kovno in Lithuania and operated around the Rudninkai forest near Vilna.

God's Underground

When foreign Jews were interned in France after the German invasion, large numbers of Christian women (most men had been sent to war) went into the camps in order to help alleviate the conditions the Jews were living in. They organized healthcare and better food. Many of these women became elements in the 'God's Underground' movement to evacuate the Jews from the camps. Children particularly were freed from the camps and found homes with Gentile families. Adults were also secretly evacuated and remained hidden for the duration of the war.

A Latvian farm worker, Yanis Lipke, regularly rescued Jews from the Riga ghetto and hid them in barns and chicken sheds belonging to his friends. In 1943 the Minsk ghetto was liquidated and a few people hid in an underground bunker. They slowly began to starve to death, until one of them set out to find food. She met Anna Dvach, who gave her food and continued to keep the 13 Jews fed for six months until the arrival of Russian troops.

Above: Father Marie Benoit, a monk from Marseilles, worked with the French Underground movement to smuggle thousands of Jewish children out of France and into Switzerland.

In Italy in 1943 a priest called Father Benoit, with the help of the Swiss, Hungarian, Rumanian and French embassies – as well as the Rome Chief of Police – helped Jews to escape the round-up by issuing false identity papers. In 1944 an Italian policeman was sent to Dachau and murdered for helping 500 Jews to get false papers and escape. In 1944 when the Kovno ghetto was liquidated, a Lithuanian carpenter called Jan Pauvlavicus built a secret hiding place in his cellar and took in about 12 Jews who he protected for three weeks until liberation. After the war he was murdered by fellow Lithuanians for helping Jews. In France Evelyne Sullerot hid 11 Jews among the mental patients that she looked after, for the duration of the war. These are just a few instances of the phenomenal acts of heroism carried out during the Holocaust.

Schindler

A German, Oscar Schindler found the war a useful way of making money, dealing on the black market and running an enamelware and munitions factory in Kracow. He employed only Jews and deliberately began making shell cases so as to have his factory designated vital to the war effort. When the Kracow ghetto was cleared, he built a special barracks for his workers close to his factory. He personally paid for his workers' food and on several occasions rescued his Jews from the transports, or in one case, hanging, risking his own survival to do so. He spent huge amounts of the factory's profits on bribing officials to keep his factory running and his Jews safe.

Left: Oscar Schindler, recognized by Israel as a Righteous (virtuous and moral) Gentile.

After the war

After the liberation, Schindler was welcomed by Jewish relief agencies and given money to start a new life in Argentina. But all his businesses failed, and in his last years Schindler returned to Europe and lived on handouts from his ever-grateful Jewish friends. After recognition in Israel for his rescue of so many Jews, he finally received a pension from the West German government in 1968. In the same year he received a Papal knighthood. In 1967 he gave evidence against some of the Germans he had dealt with in the Kracow concentration camp.

When the work camp near Kracow was closed down and his Jews were to be shipped to Auschwitz or to a labour camp, Schindler spent a small fortune bribing officials to let him take some of his Jews to a relocated factory in Brinnlitz. Schindler got 1,100 of his workers to the safety of his new factory. At one stage the women were redirected to Auschwitz and Schindler went there after them, buying them back from the commandant. By this time the war was near its end and wagonloads of dying Jews were being shunted across Poland and Germany, taking them away from the approaching Russian troops. Schindler heard about one such wagonload of dying men and arranged for them to be brought to his factory. Those still alive were put in a warm corner of the factory floor on some straw. None of them weighed more than 34 kilos – as much as a young child.

The factory never actually made a single useful shell. It had become a cover for the survival of the 1,100 Jews whom Schindler was protecting, plus the group of *Musselmen* sleeping on straw on the factory floor.

Above: The factory in Kracow where Schindler's Jews made enamelware for the German war effort.

Raoul Wallenberg

In March 1944 the Nazis occupied Hungary. Two months later the deportations of thousands of Jews to Auschwitz began even as the Russian troops advanced into Hungary from the east. In July, under increasing international pressure, the deportations were stopped. A Swedish diplomat, Raoul Wallenberg arrived in Budapest with visas for Jews to go to Sweden. The descendant of Swedish Jews, Wallenberg took over a number of houses which were given diplomatic immunity (that is, they became Swedish soil and could not be entered by Hungarians or Germans) and as many Jews as could be given visas both for Palestine and Sweden were housed in them. For a few months the war focused on other areas, and Budapest's Jews were left in relative peace. Then in October of that year an order went out for all Jews to be marched into Germany for work in munitions factories. Jews with foreign passports were to be exempted, and so Wallenberg and the Swiss consul Charles Lutz set about issuing foreign passports to as many Hungarian Jews as they could. There is a record of one passport having held as many as 957 names! By bribery, cheating, and by any official means that he could, Wallenberg issued passports and visas and even drove to catch up with one of the death marches to issue passports to men and women being marched into Germany. When Russian troops finally entered Budapest, 120,000 Jews had survived, 25,000 of them in safe houses set up by Wallenberg and other foreign officials. Wallenberg reported to the Russian authorities and was arrested as a spy. It is thought that he died in a Russian prison.

Below: Raoul Wallenberg. He was one of a few foreign officials who broke every rule to rescue Jews. Another of these men was the Japanese consul in Kovno, Lithuania, who issued visas for hundreds of people to go to Japan.

Eichmann tries to save himself

In Hungary Adolf Eichmann, one of the architects of the Final Solution, was put in charge of the evacuation of the Jews. When he saw that the war was nearly over, Eichmann offered Britain a million Jews in exchange for ten thousand trucks, which would only be used against the Russian troops, not the Western Allies. The man who negotiated with him was Saly Mayer a Swiss Jew. Mayer had no chance of actually finalizing the negotiations, since the British and Americans refused to allow anything to be paid to the Nazis, but Mayer kept up the negotiations for months, probably delaying the deportations, while Eichmann believed that exchanges might take place, but also preventing the Jews from organizing any resistance to the deportations.

Below: Adolph Eichmann awaiting trial in Israel in 1961.

Jewish efforts at rescue

Right: A French Red Cross worker helps a German prisoner of war.

Many Jews, living in disguise or hiding in woods or in some neutral country, tried rescue attempts. In Greece, which was invaded by Germany in 1941, the Jewish religious leader Rabbi Ilia Barzilai escaped from Athens to Thessaly. He actively encouraged local Jewish men not yet rounded up by the Nazis to join the resistance. He also worked with Greek resistance fighters to get 600 Jews out of Greece by boat to Turkey. Another Greek rabbi, Rabbi Pessah, arranged for 752 Jews in Volos to be hidden by local people. In Hungary a Jew called Otto Komoly got permission to set up orphanages for 5,000 Jewish children. Most of the children survived until liberation, but Komoly was shot by the SS just before the Russian troops entered the city.

Jewish partisan groups in hiding in the woods of eastern Europe made many efforts to rescue Jews from the cities. In the Nolibocka Forest in Belarus the Bielski Otriad's aim was to rescue as many Jews as possible. Once the settlement was established groups were sent into the ghettos to lead people out. The Bielski group also killed anyone who killed or betrayed Jews in hiding, making most people think carefully before committing such an act. The Bielski Otriad's group represented the largest rescue of Jews by Jews in occupied Europe.

Below: This picture was taken in 1946, and shows Rabbi Schonfeld (see page 13) with some of the children he helped to escape from Poland. He mounted a rescue operation and helped hundreds of Jews to survive the Holocaust.

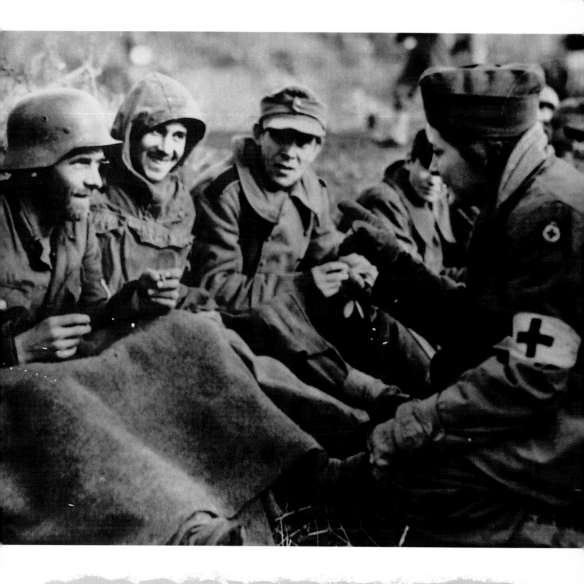

Sabina Zlatin

Sabina Zlatin was a Polish born Jewish nurse who worked with the French Red Cross for most of the war. At first she worked in Agde, a concentration camp for foreign Jews in occupied France. She and others arranged for the entire camp to be removed to a more healthy location in the Pyrenees. She got permission to take 100 children a month out of the camp and put them into quarantine before being adopted by Gentile families. In 1943 she took 17 Jewish children out of the camp and hid them in the mountains east of Lyon. The children were betrayed by an informer and taken to the death camps. Zlatin was away when the children were arrested and so survived. She rejoined the resistance, was wounded in an attack on a prison but survived the war.

Giving Testimony

In recent years hundreds of people have come forward, finally able to tell people what happened to them in the death camps, transports and ghettos. But even while the terrible events of 1939–1945 were taking place there were people who, although they could not fight, knew that they could do their bit for the Jews and others by keeping records of what went on. One of these was Emanuel Ringelbaum who began a diary of the Nazi murders as early as 1938. While he was in the Warsaw ghetto he kept records of events and endeavoured to get information to the outside world. His notes were hidden in the ghetto and recovered after his death in 1944. Like many others he might have left the ghetto and got away to safety but he felt it was his job to stay till the last. He praised the courage of the people that tried to help the Jews and kept a record of events both inside and outside the ghetto.

Left: At Babi Yar, a ravine outside Kiev, 33,000 Jews were massacred in three days. Pictured here are three survivors of the massacre visiting the memorial to this event.

Another set of records was found in the ashes of those cremated in Auschwitz. Salmen Gradowski was sent to Auschwitz in February 1943 and witnessed his family being burnt alive in the crematorium at Birkenau and was put into the sonderkommando, dragging corpses to the crematoria. He and others buried messages and records of events, as well as human teeth, in the ashes so that after the war a testimony to some of the deaths would remain. He went to the gas chamber in the autumn of 1944.

Above: This pond at Auschwitz contains the ashes of untold numbers of Jewish victims.

Salmen Gradowski

A letter, found in the ashes with the notes said: 'Dear finder, search everywhere, in every inch of soil. Tens of documents are buried under it, mine and those of other persons, which will throw light on everything that was happening here. Great quantities of teeth are also buried here. It was we, the kommando workers, who expressly have strewn them all over the terrain, as many as we could, so that the world should find material traces of the millions of murdered people. We ourselves have lost hope of being able to live to see the moment of liberation.'

(From Martin Gilbert, *The Holocaust: The Jewish Tragedy*, quoted from Jadwiga Bezwinska and Danuta Czech (eds), *Amidst a Nightmare of Crime*)

ARMED RESISTANCE

Fighting in the ghettos

M OST OF the ghetto uprisings were late on in the war. Many were tiny, with a few shots fired, a German injured and in some cases none of the Jews who witnessed them survived to tell the story. Unlike Gentile resistance groups who fought for victory, Jewish resistance was carried out by those with no hope at all for the future.

On the night of September 23, 1942 in the town of Tuczyn, Poland – home to 3,000 Jews – rebellion broke out. The Jews had been ordered to assemble at the ghetto gates the next morning. Knowing that the order meant certain death, they began to destroy the ghetto, burning anything that might be of use to the Germans. German and Ukrainian troops began to fire into the ghetto. In the confusion about 2,000 Jews escaped into the surrounding woods. Many were later rounded up and shot or surrendered to the police.

Below: In March 1942 nearly 12,000 Jews from the ghetto at Lublin, in Poland, were deported to Belzec extermination camp.

A plea from a resistance fighter.

Many ghetto Jews were reluctant to rebel, hoping that they might sit out the war and so be saved. This speech was made by one resistance leader in Vilna after hundreds of people from the Vilna ghetto had been taken to Ponar and shot:

'No-one returned of those who marched through the gates of the ghetto. All the roads of the Gestapo lead to Ponar. And Ponar means death. Those who waver, put aside all illusion. Your children, your wives, and husbands are no more. Ponar is no concentration camp. All were shot dead there. Hitler conspires to kill all the Jews of Europe, and the Jews of Lithuania have been picked at the first line. Let us not be led as sheep to the slaughter.

Brethren! Better fall as free fighters than to live at the mercy of murderers. Rise up! Rise up until your last breath.'

(Quoted in Ruby Rohrlich (ed), *Resisting the Holocaust*)

The next month in the tiny ghetto of Marcinkonis, near Grodno, Poland, 370 Jews were assembled for deportation. The Judenrat leaders suddenly called out to the assembled group to flee for their lives. Barehanded, they attacked the Nazis and while 105 died in the attack, the rest escaped into the woods.

In January 1943, several of the underground movement of Czestochowa in Poland were caught up in an unexpected deportation. One of them, Mendel Fiszlewicz, attacked and wounded the German commander. He was quickly killed. As a reprisal, 25 men were shot and 300 women and children were taken from the ghetto and sent to Treblinka death camp.

Above: The ghetto in Kracow was liquidated in March 1943. The previous December a tiny number of Jewish resistance fighters had attacked a café used by SS officers. Most were hunted down and killed.

When the ghetto of Brody was emptied in May 1943 enough ordinary Jewish people resisted the deportations to kill several Ukrainians and Germans. They had bought weapons from the Italians guarding the ghetto. The sides of the cattle trucks were beaten down by those inside and hundreds of people jumped from them either to fall under the wheels, be shot down by the guards or flee into the surrounding countryside.

The Vilna ghetto

In Vilna, Lithuania, the situation was complex. Surrounded by forests with partisan groups frequently approaching the ghetto to offer rescue, the Vilna resistance movement chose to remain in the ghetto as the protectors of the people. Ironically the people saw them as their greatest danger. The movement tried repeatedly to rouse the general population to rebellion, but were hated and accused of bringing danger to the inhabitants. When the Nazis learned the name of the leader of the underground movement, Yitzhak Wittenberg, they demanded that he be given up. The Judenrat gave him up, but the other members of the underground fought his captors and rescued him. He hid in the ghetto and terrible reprisals were threatened if he did not surrender. Wittenberg surrendered in order to stop the reprisals. He was tortured and committed suicide.

But now that the Nazis were aware of the strength of the underground they determined to liquidate the ghetto. Still rejected by the general population, the underground fled into the forests and in September 1943 the ghetto was emptied, its

Below: The Jewish Councils were often chosen by the Nazis and had to comply with their wishes. These young men and women were the staff of the Kielce ghetto in Poland.

Chaim Lazar

Chaim Lazar, a member of Vilna's underground, argued that the only hope for the ghetto dwellers was an armed rebellion. Like other members of the resistance in the Vilna ghetto he felt very bitter about the way that the other ghetto Jews had rejected their pleas for an insurrection. In his 1985 book about the ghetto and its final clearance he says:

'In the death cars, on the journey from which none returned, they would later recall how they attacked us. They would remember the stones they threw at us and the clubs they hit us with. They would recall the human sacrifice who offered himself in vain, and the blind stupidity of the fraternal war in the presence of the common enemy, and perhaps they would find atonement for their sins.'

(From Chaim Lazar, *Destruction and Resistance*, quoted in Ruby Rohrlich (ed) *Resisting the Holocaust*)

20,000 occupants going quietly to their deaths. The underground, now a partisan group in the woods, carried out attacks on German troop movements and became an important part of the partisan movement. But they were never able to defend their own community. Ironically if they had not been discovered by the Nazis the ghetto might have survived a few months longer.

Above: This picture shows Vilna today. On the eve of liberation 1,800 surviving Jews working in a factory were massacred here, in Vilna.

The Warsaw ghetto uprising

The Warsaw ghetto uprising was the most significant and well
documented of the many last desperate attempts made by Jews in
eastern Europe. When the Warsaw ghetto was first established,
all those living in it hoped that the war would end soon and they
would be liberated. Among them were tiny splinter political
groups, very young and determined not to go 'like lambs to the
slaughter'. It was many months before things became desperate
due to starvation and constant deportations to the death camps.
At this point, the underground movements were able to organize
themselves. Like the underground movements in other cities
they knew they would be fighting a hopeless war which would
end in their deaths.

Although the ghetto was officially sealed, there were many ways
of contacting the outside and gradually they persuaded the Polish
resistance to supply them with a few meagre hand guns and
grenades. Other weapons they bought on the black market in
Warsaw.

*Below: An old Jewish man
collapses on the streets of
Warsaw.*

An eyewitness account

'Though the unit was destroyed, the battle on Niska Street encouraged us. For the first time since the occupation we saw Germans clinging to the walls, crawling on the ground, running for cover, hesitating before making a step for fear of being hit by a Jewish bullet. The cries of the wounded caused us joy, and increased our thirst for battle.'

(Tuvia Borzykowski, *Between Tumbling Walls,* quoted in Martin Gilbert, *The Holocaust: The Jewish Tragedy*)

The first act of open resistance came in January 1943, when a group of Jews, including armed resistance fighters, were being deported to Treblinka death camp. Suddenly the resistance fighters, led by a man called Mordechai Anielewicz, began to throw grenades, killing some of the Germans. Most of the group were killed immediately but others barricaded themselves inside a building. The Germans brought in reinforcements and set the building on fire. Inside, those with guns continued to fire on the Germans until they were killed by German fire. A massive search of the ghetto ensued with hundreds of people randomly killed. The resistance took to the rooftops, killing Germans and taking their weapons. The fighting continued for two more days and 12 Germans were killed. Strangely, considering their enormous superiority, the Germans withdrew from the ghetto. If they had known that the resistance fighters had only a few guns and little ammunition left they would surely have continued until the last death, preventing the major rebellion the following April.

Above: As the houses in the ghetto began to burn people jumped to their deaths, avoiding the flames but being shot down in the process.

Warsaw – the final battle

The following April word spread around the Warsaw ghetto that it was about to be cleared, and its inhabitants sent to the death and slave labour camps. The resistance movement was ready for this. Hundreds of bunkers had been built for the unarmed in the hope that in the chaos they could escape through the sewers into the city. The Polish resistance had been impressed by the way that ordinary Jews had carried themselves during the previous battle, and decided to give the Jews more weapons. The Jews were armed with two submachine guns, 17 rifles and about 500 pistols, thousands of home made grenades and petrol bombs. They were outnumbered two to one by the Germans and outgunned by tanks and hundreds of machine guns. Even so the Germans were driven out of the ghetto again on the first day and 12 were killed, and their weapons were taken away. In the following days the Germans sent mortar bombs in and fired from the outside with high calibre machine guns. Buildings started to burn.

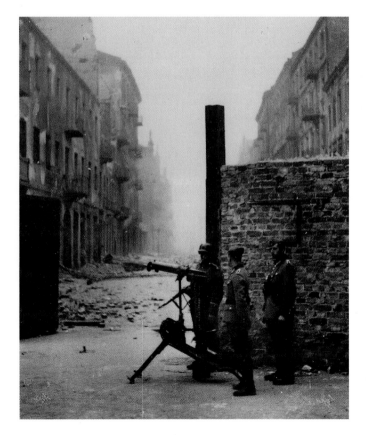

Left: From outside the ghetto walls, automatic weapons were used to kill as many people as possible.

Left: Finally the German troops were able to walk through the burning ghetto without fear of being shot at.

The battle lasted from 19 April to 16 May. Hundreds died and thousands were transported, many of them to Trawniki labour camp where they continued to resist and were killed. Several thousand probably escaped into the Aryan part of the city. People continued to hide out in bunkers in the ghetto until the following September when the ghetto was razed to the ground.

Nina Boniwna

Fourteen years old when she was caught up in the ghetto uprising in Warsaw, Nina narrowly escaped with her life. Her family was hiding in some carts to be taken to the smaller ghetto in Warsaw and they were discovered. Her mother was sent to be deported, her brother was sent to a smaller ghetto and she was lined up against a wall to be shot.

'I stood against the wall. I felt no fear at all. Everyone was flashing before my eyes, and I realized that I would never see anybody ever again.

When the man in front of me fell, I felt afraid. They shot him twice and in the end they had to finish him off with a bayonet. I was not afraid of such suffering so much as aware of the fact that none of my loved ones were with me. At the last moment a woman friend of ours shoved me onto the cart and pinned the necessary number on me, fooling the guard with her quick and unexpected action.'

Later Nina escaped from the little ghetto into Aryan Warsaw where she survived until liberation.

(Quoted in Maria Hochberg-Mariańska and Noe Grüss, *The Children Accuse*)

Bialystok

By summer 1943 most of the ghettos of eastern Europe had been emptied and their inhabitants sent to extermination centres or to work camps to die a slower death. The ghettos that remained – Lodz, Vilna, Bialystok, Czestochowa – were the largest and were decimated, the only survivors being those who could prove that they were useful workers in the local slave factories. The Warsaw ghetto uprising had been a great moral victory, but it had convinced the Germans that as the Jews became more desperate and were no longer fooled by the stories of resettlement in the east, they were becoming a danger.

In Bialystok an underground movement had also developed. Unlike other ghettos, the underground were on good terms with the Judenrat and accepted the leader's view that they should not do anything to provoke an attack on the ghetto. They agreed that they should wait until deportation was imminent before trying to fight back. When the day came in August 1943, the underground were not ready. They had a few weapons, but their plan to burn down the factories misfired and the general population went to

Below: The Polish Home Army, an underground movement, celebrating mass. At the end of the war hundreds of Jewish survivors died at the hands of Polish anti-Semites.

Bertha Sokolskaya

One of the last people to be deported from Bialystok was Bertha Sokolskaya. She was confined with 40 other people in a cattle truck. While she was in it she heard that some people from another truck had forced a way out and escaped. Weak from heat and thirst, the women in her truck decided it would be better to die.

'There was amongst us a doctor from Lodz, Chanoleskaya, who had a razor and she began slashing our wrists. We were beside ourselves, pushing and shoving and stretching out our hands. She cut one of my wrists and a fountain of blood burst out and I fell… next morning the Germans opened the door. I was still alive.'

(Quoted in Martin Gilbert, *The Holocaust:The Jewish Tragedy*)

the transports offering no resistance at all. A gun battle took place in one section of the ghetto as the young militants set fire to whatever buildings they could, in the hope that some people would escape into the woods. But none did. The resistors held out as long as they could against tanks and heavy weaponry, but eventually were defeated. A tiny number got away into the woods.

Above: In the dead of winter Jews were crowded into open trucks destined for the slave labour camps in Germany.

Jewish partisan groups

In the ghettos people chose to fight street battles with their murderers. Others chose to escape and join partisan groups. These were guerrilla movements, supporting the ideals of their own country, and in many cases nearly as anti-Semitic as the Germans. Later in the war Russia sent its own partisan groups into the woods, often dropping them by parachute.

Tuvia Bielski's group, operating in the woods of Belarus has already been mentioned in its efforts to rescue and hide Jews. In addition it was an active fighting unit, attacking German vehicles and the families of German policemen. One unit dedicated itself entirely to attacking German troops, cutting telegraph wires and fighting search parties that came into the woods.

In the Parczew forest in Poland many Jews were hiding among the trees. Many of them were dying of hunger and many had been caught in manhunts. In late 1942 a Jew called Yekhiel Grynspan escaped into the forest. Aged 24, he quickly found others who could fight. They got weapons from local Poles and spent the next two years, until Soviet troops infiltrated the woods and took command – attacking German and Ukrainian police posts, and even setting fire to the German police headquarters in Parczew town.

In May 1942, Moyshe Gildeman established a Jewish partisan group in Volhynia, sabotaging railway lines and storage depots.

Left: Fourth from the left in this picture is Yekhiel Grynspan, with other Jewish partisans. They had escaped from the trains taking Jews to Sobibor extermination camp. They protected Jewish refugees in the Parczew forest in Poland.

In January 1943 they were accepted into the Soviet partisan army as a special Jewish unit. Another Jewish group led by Haim Henry Rozenson joined the same group. Another group in White Russia, led by Abba Kovner who had escaped with other underground members from the Vilna ghetto, destroyed two bridges and two railway engines, as well as many telegraph poles. Many more small fighting units perished in battles with the German troops.

Left: The Vilna partisans return to the ghetto after liberation in July 1944. Vitka Kempner is at the far right and Abba Kovner is fourth from the right. They married after the war.

Vitka Kempner

An underground member in the Vilna ghetto in 1943, Vitka blew up a German military train and escaped back to the ghetto. Two months later she blew up a transformer inside Vilna then got into the nearby labour camp and smuggled out several dozen prisoners. Later in the war she joined a partisan group and burned down a turpentine factory in the town of Olkiniki. A survivor, Hava Shurek describes seeing Vitka after she had blown up the train:

'There was a strength in her eyes which gave them an unusual brightness... When she was asked what she had thought during the long night, she answered: "How to do the job without falling into their hands..." (The Germans) did not suspect the Jews, for they were sure that the Jews were already defeated and would not raise their heads. Such a deed could only be done by free men.'

(Quoted in Martin Gilbert, *The Nazi Holocaust: The Jewish Tragedy* from the *Kalish Book*)

Armed resistance and escape attempts in the camps

By the time most people arrived in the death camps or the work camps they had endured months of starvation, the loss of their families, transportation and illness. The fact that any rebellions at all took place in these camps is remarkable. The attacks rarely resulted in anything more than the deaths of the people who made them.

In 1942, when the labour camp at Kruszyna was being liquidated, the Jews attacked their guards with knives and fists. Six died but four escaped. On the way to the transports more resistance resulted in the deaths of those who refused to board the cattle trucks. Three weeks later the labour camp near Minsk in Belarus was emptied and again the inmates resisted, barricading themselves inside a building which was burned to the ground with 400 people inside. In August 1943, At Babi Yar, in the suburbs of Kiev, 400 Jews and Soviet POWs were forced to open mass graves and burn the corpses. (The Germans had begun to fear that the war might end in defeat for them and that there would be retribution for their treatment of the Jews. All over

Below: In the ghettos disease and malnutrition killed many people.

Sobibor

One of the more successful armed breakouts took place at Sobibor in 1943. There were 600 Jews in the labour camp, many of them teenagers. Led by a Jewish Red Army POW they planned a breakout. Girls working in the staff quarters stole weapons and knives, and hatchets were made. Warm clothing was hidden ready for escape. On October 13, the Jews were ready. Weapons were distributed and the order was given. Nine SS men and two Ukrainians were killed and 300 people escaped into the woods. The rest were killed. About ten of those who escaped survived the war.

Left: This memorial was erected to the victims of the Babi Yar massacre.

German occupied eastern Europe records and corpses were being destroyed.) They worked in inhuman conditions, wearing shackles. Executions took place at random. As they hauled the rotting corpses out of the mass graves, the Jews searched them for keys, hoping that they might find one to fit the bunker that they were locked up in each night. Miraculously, such a key was found and 325 Jews and POWs escaped. 311 were shot down as they ran but 14 escaped, ten of them surviving the war.

Treblinka

At Treblinka death camp there were several planned attempts at armed breakouts. In 1943 a Jewish doctor, Julian Chorazycki, found a Ukrainian guard who was willing to supply weapons for cash. The money was stolen from Jewish confiscated goods and several weapons came into Jewish hands. But in April of that year Chorazycki was discovered and took poison, having first wounded the SS officer who exposed him. In June of that year, 40 hand grenades were smuggled into the camp but were defective. In August the inmates broke into the camp arsenal (weapon store-room) and stole 40 guns and some grenades. At the same time the huts were sprayed with petrol. At a given signal the huts were lit and the rebellion began. Sixteen guards were killed and 150 people escaped. The rest of the 700 camp inmates were killed. The camp was evacuated in that year and the remaining prisoners were given the task of destroying the evidence. Thirteen of them were working outside the fence when one, Seweryn Klajnman aged 18, killed the guard, put on his uniform and marched the others away from the camp. All 13 escaped.

Right: A reconstruction at Auschwitz of the crematorium ovens. The originals were destroyed immediately after liberation.

Below: Treblinka death camp as it looks today.

Revolt at Auschwitz-Birkenau

In 1943, at Birkenau a group of women destined for the gas chambers rebelled after one, whose surname only survives, Horowitz, grabbed a gun and shot two guards. The women took her action as a stimulus and attacked the guards, tearing off the nose of one and scalping another. All the women were shot. One of the guards that Horowitz had shot was well known for strangling Jews with his bare hands. He died of his wounds. The next year a revolt took place among the 500 sonderkommando, all Greek Jews who had watched their families killed. Some girls working in the munitions factory stole explosives for them. At a roll call, one of the sonderkommando attacked the guards with his bare hands, ran to crematorium IV and packed the explosives into it. The crematorium exploded. When other groups saw the crematorium ablaze they used the chaos to cut the fence and ran. Most were cut down by machine gun fire, but 12 escaped and remained at large for a few hours before being shot. The girls who had stolen the explosives were discovered and tortured before execution. All 600 sonderkommando were executed in the wake of the rebellion – except for three doctors, one of whom, a man called Nyiszli, survived to tell the story. Of all the violent rebellions in the camps, this was the only one which actually damaged the Nazi war machine by putting one of the crematoria out of action.

Mala and Edek

Caught up in the Nazi trap when Germany invaded Belgium, Mala Zimetbaum, aged 20, found herself in Auschwitz working as a runner taking messages from one part of the vast camp complex to another. This was a very useful job and Mala often found out information which she was able to pass on to prisoners to help them. She was a very popular person and everyone in the camp was pleased when she and her lover Edek Galiski escaped, disguised as an SS officer and a prisoner. Edek had stolen the uniform and Mala had stolen the pass.

Various stories have been told about how they were recaptured, but they were at large for several weeks before they were brought back into the camp. Mala was tortured and taken to be hanged in front of the assembled women of Auschwitz. Before they could kill her, she cut her wrists and was hauled off to the crematorium. Edek similarly refused to be murdered by throwing himself into the noose and kicking loose the stool he was standing on, before the hanging could be done officially. Many Auschwitz survivors tell this story about two people's escape and re-arrest. It stands out as a triumph of young lovers against the

Left: The barbed wire fences are a reminder of the horrors that went on in Auschwitz and its satellite camps.

vast Nazi machine. Even though they died they had still had a few weeks together on the outside, and they took their own lives rather than allowing the Nazis to murder them. The significance of their escape can be seen in the fact that the Germans didn't kill them on the spot, a fate suffered by countless thousands of runaway Jews – but brought them back to the camp to show the other prisoners that there was no escape.

Above: Older women and children were selected to go to the gas chambers. These people were probably dead within hours of this picture being taken.

Reactions to the escape

Fania Fenelon, a member of the Auschwitz orchestra, recalls how she felt when Mala and Edek escaped:

'We were insanely gleeful. Our reasoning was over-simple but heartening: Since they're out, we'll be freed. We were beside ourselves... We could already see Mala and Edek returning at the head of millions of soldiers, who would enter the camp and put out the SS men's eyes, bayonet them in the stomach. We were drunk with images of gory revenge. For the first time since our internment we lived and breathed hope... There were vicious searches throughout the camps, interrogations in the SS building, accomplices were sought. But everyone claimed ignorance and it was true.'

(From Fania Fenelon, *Playing for Time*, quoted in Otto Friedrich, *The Kingdom of Auschwitz*)

LIKE LAMBS TO THE SLAUGHTER?

UNTHINKING PEOPLE often ask why so many Jewish people went to their deaths without a struggle, 'like lambs to the slaughter'. The stories here, and the many hundreds of others, show that Jews and others did fight to save Jewish lives. During the war thousands of people – Soviet POWs, strong young men, Communists, homosexuals and gypsies – also tragically went to their deaths in the camps. The Nazi war machine made resistance a superhuman effort and it is all the more remarkable that anyone was able to fight back.

By the time that the liquidation of the ghettos began, most young people had been taken to work camps and a large proportion of those that remained were the elderly, sick or children. Hardly the most likely people to take up arms, even if they could.

Those who did take up arms did so under the most difficult circumstances. Jewish underground groups had little support from Polish or Russian partisans, no assistance from the western Allied forces, no weapons except those that they could steal or make themselves, no strength on a starvation diet and unhealthy

Left: German children playing happily in the years before the Holocaust. These may well have been the adults who turned their backs while their Jewish neighbours went to the ghettos.

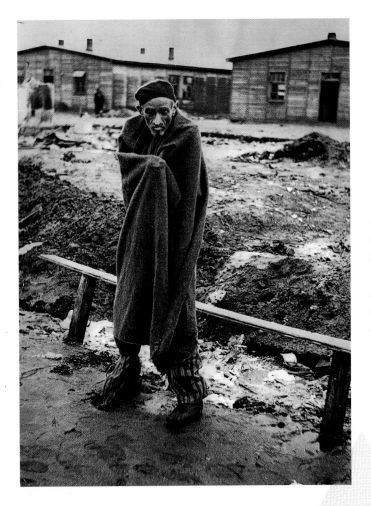

Left: An inmate of Bergen-Belsen concentration camp – a Hungarian Jew sent to Belsen as a political prisoner. Hunger, inhuman working conditions and brutal treatment took their toll on his health.

living conditions. They also faced the violent opposition of the ghetto Jews.

Worse still perhaps was the inability to overcome the belief that nothing as insane as the Holocaust could possibly be happening in a modern, civilized society. The Jews in the ghettos, where resistance should have been the greatest, had no contact with the outside world. They had no evidence, besides some rumours that the mass murders were taking place, and were daily persuaded by the Nazis that all would be well if they would just co-operate. After years of anti-Semitic abuse, of being told that they were less than human, a disease, a threat to society, they had been made to feel isolated, helpless and ashamed. Such feelings could often prove to be stronger than the anger and injustice felt at what was happening to them.

The Survivors

Who were the survivors?

A larger proportion of people who took action to save themselves survived than those who chose inaction. Because emigration and hiding were expensive and only available to a limited number of people, poorer people, or those in Poland, had less chance of taking this option. On the other hand, in the early days of Hitler's rise to power many wealthy people chose to stay rather than abandon everything that they had in Germany.

Below: Few of the millions who died had their ashes treated this carefully. This is an official SS photograph from Theresienstadt, a ghetto which the Germans attempted to turn into a model settlement and allowed the Red Cross to visit.

• Because of the selection process at the camps, few children under the age of ten, elderly people, people with disabilities or women with small children survived the war.
• Some wealthy or prominent Jews were sent to Bergen Belsen, a model camp where the living although harsh was not deadly. Many survived.
• Some Hungarian Jews survived because Hungary was invaded late on in the war and the killing machine just didn't have time to get to them.

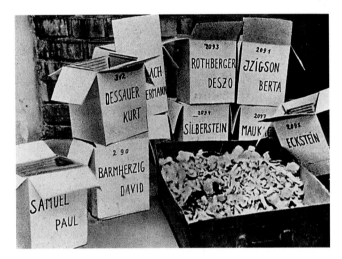

A buried message from one of the sonderkommando

'And there a girl of five stood and undressed her brother who was one year old. One from the kommando came to take off the boy's clothes. The girl shouted loudly "Be gone, you Jewish murderer! Don't lay your hands, dripping with Jewish blood upon my lovely brother! I am his good mummy, he will die in my arms together with me." A boy of seven or eight stood beside her and spoke thus, "Why, you are a Jew and you lead such dear children to the gas chamber – only in order to live? Is your life among the band of murderers really dearer to you than the lives of so many Jewish victims?" '

(Quoted in Martin Gilbert, *The Holocaust:The Jewish Tragedy*)

• Danish and Norwegian Jews survived because of public attempts to help them.
• Finnish and Italian Jews survived because their governments refused to give them up.
• Others, in the death camps survived because their strength of will, religious beliefs or sense of survival made it possible.
• For others the expression that one survivor used, 'tainted luck', is the only reason that they survived. They just happened not to die.

In general the massive killing machine invented by the Nazis for ridding Europe of people they considered unworthy of life was very efficient. Those who survived their onslaught did so because of minor inefficiencies of the system, as well as through enormous courage and resourcefulness.

Left: In modern Warsaw the ghetto area is now a series of housing estates, but there are many memorials (in Polish and English, not Yiddish) marking key spots in the defence of the ghetto.

DATELINE

1939
September Einsatzgruppen begin mass exterminations in Poland.
December Labour camps set up throughout Poland. All Jewish males required for forced labour.

1940
May Lodz ghetto sealed off.
October Deportations to the Warsaw ghetto begin.
October Foreign Jews interned in Vichy France.

1941
February Deportations of Dutch Jews to German concentration camps.
June Invasion of Soviet Union. Einsatzgruppen massacres extend to Baltic states and western Ukraine.
September Construction of Birkenau death camp begins.
December Gas vans begin operation at Chelmno.

1942
January Resistance movement begins to organize itself in Vilna.
March First transports of Polish Jews to the death camps.
July Mass deportations of Dutch Jews to Auschwitz.
July Deportations begin in Warsaw.
October Deportations of Jews from Norway. Many escape.
November Deportations begin in Bialystok region, Poland.
November German Gypsies deported to Auschwitz.

1943
March Deportations of Greek Jews to Auschwitz.
March Kracow ghetto closed. Schindler's Jews move into his factory site.
April–May Warsaw ghetto uprising.
May Shmuel Zygielbojm commits suicide in London.
June Lwow ghetto liquidated.
August Attempted breakout from Treblinka.
August Bialystok ghetto cleared. Attempted revolt put down.
September Danish Jews ferried to safety in Sweden.
September Vilna ghetto liquidated.
October Breakout from Sobibor.
October Deportations of Italian Jews to Auschwitz.

1944
May Deportations of Hungarian Jews begin.
July Death marches begin, Majdanek death camp liberated by Red Army.
August Lodz ghetto liquidated.
October Inmates blow up one of the crematoria at Auschwitz.
November Wallenberg intercedes on behalf of Hungarian Jews.
November Gas chambers destroyed at Auschwitz by the Nazis.

1945
January Death marches out of Poland into Germany.
January Auschwitz liberated.
May Germany surrenders. Jews continue to die in German concentration camps, now all liberated.

FURTHER READING

Ruby Rohrlich (ed.), *Resisting the Holocaust*, Berg, 1998

Nathan Stoltzfus, *Resistance of the Heart*, W W Norton & Co. New York, 1996

Martin Gilbert, *Never Again: A History of the Holocaust*, HarperCollins, 2000

The Diary of Anne Frank, Vallentine Mitchell, 1953

Maria Hochberg-Mariañska and Noe Grüss, *The Children Accuse*, Vallentine Mitchell, 1996

Thomas Keneally, *Schindler's Ark*, Hodder & Stoughton, 1975

R G Grant, *The Holocaust: New Perspectives*, Wayland, 1997

Clive A Lawson, *The Story of the Holocaust*, Franklin Watts, 2000

INTERNET SITES

http://www.vhf.org/

Survivors of the Shoah Visual History Foundation. It has photographs and stories by survivors.

http://www.ushmm.org/

The website of the United States Holocaust Memorial Museum in Washington. A pictorial history of the Holocaust.

http://www.yad-vashem.org.il/

The website for Yad Vashem – the Holocaust Martyrs' and Heroes' Remembrance Authority.

http://www.iwm.org.uk/

The website of the Imperial War Museum in London.

SOURCES

The quotations in this book were taken from:

Samuel Pisar, *Of Blood and Hope*, London, 1980

Maria Hochberg-Mariañska and Noe Grüss, *The Children Accuse*, Vallentine Mitchell, 1996

The Diary of Anne Frank, Vallentine Mitchell, 1953

Lucy Dawidowitz, *The War against the Jews*, Penguin, 1990

Ruby Rohrlich (ed), *Resisting the Holocaust*, 1998

Martin Gilbert, *The Holocaust: The Jewish Tragedy*, Fontana, 1987

Jadwiga Bezwinska and Danuta Czech (eds), *Amidst a Nightmare of Crime : Manuscripts of Members of Sonderkommando*, Oswiecim, 1973

Chaim Lazar, *Destruction and Resistance*, Shengold New York, 1985

Tuvia Borzykowski, *Between Tumbling Walls*, Tel Aviv, 1972

Fania Fenelon (trans. Judith Landry), *Playing for Time*, Atheneum, 1977

Michael Marrus, *The Holocaust in History*, Penguin, 1987

PLACES TO VISIT

The Imperial War Museum in London has an exhibition dedicated to the Holocaust.

Imperial War Museum, Lambeth Road, London, SE1 6HZ, United Kingdom, 020 7416 5320.

Holocaust Centre, Beth Shalom, Laxton, Newark, Nottinghamshire NG22 0PA. (Telephone bookings and information: 01623 836627; email: office@bethshalom.com). Not suitable for children under 11.

GLOSSARY

anti-semitism prejudice against Jewish people.

Aryan in Nazi ideology, a white skinned northern European, not of Jewish descent.

atonement a way of seeking forgiveness for a sin.

Auschwitz–Birkenau the major killing centre in the Nazi empire. It extended over several miles and included satellite work camps besides the three main camps Auschwitz I the original work camp, Birkenau, the extermination camp and Monowitz the industrial centre.

Babi Yar a ravine on the outskirts of Kiev in the Ukraine, where approximately 33,000 Jews were murdered by the Einsatzgruppen.

Baumgruppe a group of partisans who operated in Berlin after 1941, and partly destroyed an anti-Soviet exhibit in the city.

Belarus a small country between Poland and Russia in Europe.

communism the theory that all property should be state-owned and that each person should be paid according to his or her needs.

concentration camps detention camps for the enemies of the Nazi state. Set up in 1933, they involved forced labour. Extended throughout the Nazi empire to hold chiefly, but not only, Jews.

consuls officials who work for their country in a foreign city to protect their fellow citizens in that country.

cyanide of potassium a poison.

Dachau a concentration camp in Germany, one of the first to be set up.

decimate to kill or destroy a group of people or animals.

dehumanize to deprive people of basic human rights so that they feel inferior and weakened.

death camps centres where Jews, Gypsies and homosexuals were sent to be murdered. The chief death camps were all in Poland: Auschwitz-Birkenau, Belzec, Chelmno, Majdanek, Sobibor and Treblinka.

death marches the forced evacuation of camp inmates in the final stages of the war.

Einsatzgruppen special mobile units responsible for large-scale massacres of Poles, Russian Jews, Communists and intellectuals.

extermination the destruction of a living thing.

Fascist originally the name of an extreme right wing nationalist group established in Italy in the 1920s, the term is now applied to all political parties of a nationalist, racist and extreme right wing nature.

Final Solution the Nazi term for the mass murder of Jews, Gypsies, homosexuals, Jehovah's Witnesses and other minorities.

fraternal brotherly feeling. It refers to a group of people with common interests, like the Jews in a particular ghetto.

Gentiles non-Jews.

ghettos a very run-down area where Jews were forced to live during periods of the Second World War.

Hanukkah the Jewish festival of light, commemorating the purification of the temple in 165 BC.

insurrection an uprising or armed rebellion against authority.

Judenrat 'Jewish Council', the representative body established by the Nazis in the ghettos. They administered Nazi decrees.

kapos Nazi appointed overseers in the camps, usually German criminals rather than Jews.

labour camp a camp dedicated to the German war effort, using Jews, POWs, and other citizens of occupied states.

liquidate to kill something.

Lwow (Lvov) a town in Lithuania with a large ghetto population.

Mischling half or quarter Jews, some of whom were allowed to stay in Germany.

Musselmen people who were so near to death that they had given up all sense of their own identity and wandered around in a daze.

Nazi Party (Nationalsozialistische Deutsche Arbeiterpartei) in English 'National Socialist German Workers' Party'. Led by Hitler, the Nazi Party governed Germany between 1933 and 1945.

partisans underground freedom fighters that fought against the Germans, not necessarily on behalf of the Jews.

pogrom mass murder of people by a mob of their fellow citizens. The term usually applies to the attacks on Jews.

resistance (French) an organization that is fighting secretly within an occupied country for liberation (freedom).

Shoah Hebrew for Holocaust.

sonderkommando a special squad whose job it was to lead people to the gas chambers and then dispose of the bodies.

Theresienstadt a model concentration camp near Prague created in November 1941 and used to allay Western suspicions about the fate of the Jews.

Untermenschen in Nazi ideology, sub-humans, or people of inferior race.

Vichy France a German-controlled French government set up in Southern France after the German conquest.

White Russia another name for Belarus, a country in Europe.

INDEX